The Pursuit *of* Happiness

21 Spiritual Rules To Success

D1531381

Jennifer O'Neill

Second Print Edition: April 2018

Information provided in this material should not be relied upon as a substitute for advice, programs, or treatment that you would normally receive from a licensed professional, such as a lawyer, doctor, psychiatrist, financial adviser, or any other licensed professional.

Table of Contents

Spiritual Rule #1
Understand You Are a Reflection of Your Choices

"Blaming is so much easier than taking responsibility, because if you take responsibility ...then you might be to blame."

I want you to take a moment and give some thought to the people who surround you, the people who are currently in your life right now. Observe them for a minute. It might be a member of your family, friends, or coworkers, whomever you choose. I want you to observe his or her life, with no attachment and no judgment on your part. Now think about it, these people are clearly a reflection of the choices they have made in their life so far. They are in their current situation because of all of the choices they have made in their lifetime, and those choices have helped to contribute to where they are at today. Some of the choices they have made have most likely been good, and some of them no doubt have been bad, but they all had "choices." You are also a reflection of the accumulation of choices that you have made throughout your lifetime. The wonderful and most amazing thing about this is that you do indeed have choices. In fact, you have many choices, every single day. The downside is you must also take responsibility for the choices you make. The ones you have made up until this point, and the ones you continue to make, every single day.

Now, you may wonder, "How does this correlate to my own life exactly?" Well, here are some examples. Were you a teen parent? Did you finish high school or go to college? Did you pursue what it is that you love doing most in life? Or did you settle because that's what everyone else did? Did you marry for love? Did you stay for the kids? These are all choices, and choices that may have very clearly defined your life in some way.

Everyone has issues they need to work through, and even overcome; no one is immune to problems. It doesn't matter who you are, where you work, or if you work, it is something we all have in common as human beings. How we choose to deal with these issues, however, is what sets people apart; that is the difference.

> *"It's not about if you have chaos in your life,*
> *it's about how well you manage it."*

When people are unhappy, they blame many other things. They blame the economy, the government, their health, their spouse or significant other, their parents, their childhood, you name it … there is definitely something beyond their control causing their unhappiness, because they would not be in their current situation by choice! That would be ridiculous! Or would they?

There are some very successful people in the world who will settle for nothing short of success! They work and they plan, they fail and they overcome, but they will succeed. There are also some people who never seem to be able to get it together. They self-sabotage, they are broke, they are unhappy, and they never (they believe) ever seem to be able to catch a break. They will continue to make choices over and over that will match who they believe they are, because your choices are very much a reflection of your personality.

Take a minute to answer these questions about yourself, truthfully:

1) What do you think other people see when they look at you?
2) Does it reflect your personality?
3) Does it match who you want to be?
4) What choices have you made to contribute to where you are at currently in life?

This is just a series of questions to help you to expand your mind and shift your perspective. You have so many wonderful choices in life; however, many times people do not see it that way. They *choose* to see it another way, the way in which they have no choice. You can look at it this way if you wish, but it is simply not true; you always have a choice, so own up to the choices you make. Now, some of the choices you have made in life may have been good choices, and some of them may have been bad choices, but that really doesn't matter anymore ... what matters is NOW!

How to make choices that work for you:

1) You are no longer a victim; you are a choice maker!

Start seeing yourself that way and take responsibility for the choices you are making from here on out. If you want to lose weight, stop eating unhealthy foods. If you are unhappy, figure out what choices you are making that are contributing to your unhappiness. There are no excuses here; if you don't like what's happening, fix it. If you don't want to fix it, then don't complain about it!

2) Make choices that are in alignment with who you are and where you want to see yourself in the future.

This is very *important!* Stop making choices that are not in alignment with who you are, period! This causes resistance and resentment. It makes you bitter and uncomfortable when you make choices that do not align with who you are, but most people do it anyway. Many times people feel their own discomfort is less important than someone else's comfort. This is trained behavior, drilled into us at a young age. You are considered "selfish" if you put your own comfort or happiness in front of someone else's comfort or happiness. Selfishness is ludicrous! "How dare you not help me feel better first!" That seems a bit hypocritical if you ask me. Especially since it is not possible to make other people happy (see spiritual rule #5), if this is being selfish, by all means, be selfish! Of course, I am not talking about completely ignoring the wants and needs of those around us, or causing someone intentional harm. However, you cannot help someone else who is not willing to help themselves. In order to help those who are willing to help themselves effectively, you must be coming from a place of fulfillment and happiness.

3) Own the power of choice!

Take your head out of the sand! It is time to recognize that you, and you alone, have a tremendous amount of power over who you are. No one else holds this power over you, unless of course, you *choose* to give up this power to him or her. Understand that ultimately you are the final decision maker in your own life. There is no one to blame; you are the CEO in charge!

You can try and figure out how this rule does not apply to you, and you can go about your day feeling sad, depressed, and hopeless. Or you can choose to change what you don't like. The wonderful thing is, it's your choice!

You are never stuck, unless you are choosing to stay there.

You are never limited, unless you choose to limit yourself.

You are never less than, unless you choose to see yourself this way.

You will never fail, unless you choose failure as an option.

You are powerful beyond belief!

Spiritual Rule #2
Do Not Let Your Relationship Status Define Your Happiness

"You cannot borrow half of who you are from someone else, yet people try to do it all of the time, they just call it a relationship!"

This is a very common mistake people make, attaching their happiness to their relationship status. If you are unhappy right now, and say that you don't do this ... well, I don't believe you! You've heard it a million times before, "This is my better half," or "They complete me!" It has become an accepted way of thinking in society today, and it is causing a huge problem. People think it is natural, or common, to feel "whole" when you are in a relationship, in fact, they do not even think twice about it! Society has adapted the mind-set that wholeness and relationships are linked, they have unknowingly blended the two together. The problem is, you cannot borrow half of who you are from someone else, and this is exactly what you are trying to do when you feel this way! As a result, people have become very focused on being in a relationship, because they like the way they *feel* when they are in one. What they don't pay attention to is what they are actually experiencing. Distraction!

"What?" I am sure you are wondering, "How does that work?" Well, it's really pretty easy. Whenever you do not *feel whole* you are experiencing what is called a spiritual void. This spiritual void happens when your soul is being malnourished in a sense. You are not fulfilling yourself on a soul level (in other words, you are breaking many of the rules in this book.) When your soul is malnourished this feeling becomes very noticeable, and many times, it is mistaken for loneliness. How does this involve your relationship? When you are in a relationship, most people no longer notice the void, another person is essentially distracting them. You become more focused on what this other person is doing, and what they are doing now, and now, you get the drift. When another person becomes such a focus in your life, under these circumstances, your happiness meter begins to fluctuate with their behavior. Your happiness then becomes attached to your significant other and your relationship. Of course, it is natural to have things in your relationship affect your happiness from time to time, for a "temporary" time period. In fact, there is no way to avoid it. When you are arguing, or going through a stressful time in your life or in your relationship, your happiness can become affected. What I am talking about here is becoming so focused on your relationship status, that your relationship's effect on your happiness is not temporary, but permanent! Now, I have broken this down into two different categories for you, so here they are:

If You Are In a Relationship

If you are in a relationship and your partner seems to have a HUGE impact on your day-to-day happiness. (Now, I do not expect you to know this if you are one of these people, but your friends will, so ask them.) If your friends constantly complain to you, and say things like, "You will never be happy with so and so," or they are tired of hearing you complain to them about your relationship, there is a problem. Just to reiterate, there will be days when you and your significant other will argue, or whatever, and it will affect your happiness (temporarily), and that is normal. But when you are experiencing a spiritual void and do not feel whole yourself and you do not have anything else going on in your life to focus upon that is good for you, your primary focus *will* become your relationship. Your focus will become your partner and what your partner is doing. Every move they make will give you a mood swing.

If You Are Not In a Relationship

If you are not in a relationship and you only seem to be happy when you are in one, this is a big problem! Yes it is normal to be lonely (to an extent), yes it is normal to want a companion, but it is not ~~normal~~ (it is absurd how many people think this is normal so I *choose* to use a different word here), it is not "healthy" to feel happy only when you are in a relationship. This is in fact a huge red flag that you have a spiritual void going on in your life that you need to fill!

How do you fill spiritual void?

Start with Spiritual Rules #6, #10 and #15 right away!

Spiritual Rule #3
Remove All Contingency Clauses Attached To Your Happiness!

"When working with the Universal Laws you are working with the laws of manifestation, not instant gratification ..."

People have become very spoiled. I would go so far as to say, in many instances, that adults many times behave like spoiled children! As the world has become more materialistic, so have humans. Materialism has begun to overwhelm the physical senses. Materialism is a big contributing factor to people placing contingency clauses on their happiness, and the funny thing is, they do not even know they are doing it unless it is brought to their attention. However, from this day forward, understand since this has now been brought to your attention, you may no longer use this as an excuse!

I hate to break the news to you, but as humans, we are fickle people. As fickle people here is the problem: when one thing on your "I will be happy when list" gets crossed off, another item will promptly take its place, then another, then another, and so on. If you are thinking, "I don't do this!" not so fast. The tricky part here is, most of the people who do this (and it is a lot of people), *do not notice* that they are doing it. Because it is another "accepted" way of thinking by society today, so it has made this thought process very easily disguisable.

Do you do any of these things?

1) Do you think about retiring often and how nice it will be?
2) Are you aggravated at work and often wish you worked somewhere else?
3) Do you wish you lived somewhere else?
4) Do you wish you had a different car, house, etcetera?
5) Do you live beyond your means?
6) Do you wish you were in/out of a relationship often?

If you answer yes to three or more of these questions, you have most likely adapted very well to this thought process. Most likely, without knowing it, you have probably been placing contingency clauses on your happiness.

What contingency clauses have you knowingly or unknowingly placed on your happiness?

Now that this has been brought to your attention, I want you to think about this question for a minute. Here are some examples to help get you started: When I get out of this place, I will be happy. When I get a better job, I will be happy. When I can retire, I will be happy. When I can purchase XYZ, I will be happy. Try and think of as many contingency clauses you have placed (knowingly or unknowingly) on your happiness, as you can. Why?

Because it raises your awareness … and awareness is key to changing this behavior!

When you become more aware of this type of thinking it becomes a habit that you can easily break. But most likely you may not have been aware of it until now. You may also be surprised at how often you find yourself, or other people, thinking this way. When you remove contingency clauses attached to your happiness, it will force your attention into "the now" and finding joy today. This simple action is helping you to find happiness within the life you have already created, your life as it is today, not your life as you hope it will be tomorrow.

Spiritual Rule #4
Release Yourself From Expectations

"Do you see the people in your life for who they really are, or do you see them how you want them to be? Never keep someone in your life because you are expecting them to change, keep them in your life because you appreciate them regardless of change!"

An expectation is a *belief* that there will be a certain outcome in the future, which may or may not be realistic. A *belief* is when you have faith or confidence, that something is fact or true, without substantial proof. Expectations usually involve another person, or people, or an outcome of a situation, oftentimes resulting in disappointment.

Wow! I bet you never realized how complicated having an expectation could be. Expectations are extremely toxic to your happiness!

Problems with expectations:

#1 Element of control

When people have placed an expectation on someone or something, it is usually because they want to *control* what the outcome essentially is. When an expectation is placed, there is *resistance* to any other outcome than what is "expected." You have decided this is the only acceptable outcome (otherwise, there would be no expectation.)

#2 Belief

Belief means that you "believe" there will be a certain outcome in the future, which may or may not be realistic, without substantial proof! The crazy thing about this is you have no substantial proof that things are going to turn out the way you expect them to, yet you are still "expecting" it to turn out the way in which you "believe" it will. One of the greatest things about the future is that the future is constantly changing. However, that also makes it hard to anticipate a certain outcome.

#3 Disappointment

When you become rigid in your thinking, you have a very high probability of disappointment. The act of feeling disappointment itself is not the whole problem, but the resistance that you feel in the body as a result of acquiring an expectation is. Resistance and other negative feelings felt energetically in the body, such as disappointment, can and do cause illness.

Releasing yourself from expectations:

1)   Release yourself from your own expectations.

This is going to be hard for many people and yet one of the most freeing things that you will ever experience. Stop expecting others to behave differently! Why? *Because you cannot control other people's behavior!* Period! I don't care how hard you try, the illusion that you can control another person's behavior is just that, an illusion. I don't care if the other person is two years old or eighty-two years old, they choose to react to you, or a situation, all on their own. Now you can "wish" they behave differently, but do not expect it. The best thing you can do for yourself is to accept other people's behavior and the choices they make. You may not agree with them, you may even wish them to do things differently, but accept it. Just as you would appreciate other people accepting the choices that you make.

2)   Release yourself from expectations that other people put on you.

All people put expectations on someone or something in order to reduce the anxiety, fear, or worry that they have within themselves. They want to feel calm inside, and in order to do that, many people "mistakenly" think that the calmness comes from outside of themselves. So they do their best to control their environment. The problem with this is that you may be "in their environment." So do not alter what is best for you in order to calm someone else's environment. Because you do not have that much control over their environment!

"Control is an illusion. You will never be able to control anything, any situation, or anyone without consent. So in actuality there is no control, there is only consent!"

Spiritual Rule #5
Do Not Hold Anyone Else Responsible For Your Happiness

"You would not want to be responsible for someone else's happiness, so please do not hold someone else responsible for yours!"

This is going to be a challenge for many people! But the challenge is not without its rewards!

Today I would like you to commit to taking COMPLETE responsibility for your own happiness!!!

I bet some of you are almost laughing thinking, "Are you kidding? That's it? This will be easy." Well good, then you should welcome the challenge!

How relieved would you feel if you knew that no one, and I mean no one, could affect your happiness? Your happiness was perfectly preserved inside of yourself, protected from all of the negativity that flourishes in the world outside of yourself. Not a single soul could taint your happiness, not your spouse, not your kids, your parents, or your boss, no one! Just bask in that feeling for a minute … doesn't it feel nice? Don't you almost feel lighter knowing that other people cannot affect your happiness? Well, this might be your lucky day because this is reality. Most likely, up until this point your perception has probably been different, that your happiness is vulnerable. You see, people react to other people all day long; you react to someone's tone of voice, their facial expressions, their body language, etcetera. You even react to situations that you are in, so a large portion of your day is actually spent reacting to other people's be-haviors. Reaction should not define your happiness, and it is really energy wasted. You might be thinking, "I am not into drama, I don't do this. But I know people who do." Well let me assure you, everyone does this! The key here is to be aware of it, and keep your reactions to other people's thoughts and actions in perspective. I have put together some steps for you to try and keep things in perspective.

1) Meditation/Visualization

I like to start my day with a visualization technique. It is kind of like a mini meditation, and I would like you to try it. You start out by finding a comfortable chair to sit in, and relax your body completely. However, instead of going into a deep meditation, I want you to spend some time visualizing your day. In order to utilize this visualization technique at its most effective level, I do not want you to visualize how the day's events are going to go, only concentrate on visualizing yourself and how you feel at the end of the day. See yourself feeling wonderful and satisfied on how the day's events unfolded. Do not go over any particulars, only concentrate on the happy, satisfied "feeling" that you are experiencing. Imagine yourself reflecting on your day after dinner and saying to yourself, "What a great day!" *It is important not go over any details*, just concentrate on how you feel at the end of the day. Imagine that you feel lighter, and happy about the daily events. Do this in the morning.

2) Release Expectations

Since we just went over this in chapter four, you should have a good handle on how this works. Today I want you to throw all of the expectations that you have placed on others out the window. You may not punish anyone, by anger, the silent treatment, or whatever, for not living up to expectations that YOU have set for them. Expectations are way too common and you definitely set yourself up for disappointment when you have them. The funny thing is, most of the time people do not even tell other people what their expectations are of them! They just take for granted that there are a lot of mind readers out there. Now that is definitely setting someone up to fail!

3) Stop Taking Things So Personally

For today, keep your emotions in check by not reacting negatively, or responding in anger, to someone else having a bad day. People who are having a bad day like to spread it around and you may be in the crossfire! Do not *allow* them to affect your happiness. Even if you feel that it is directed at you (usually it is because you are at the wrong place at the wrong time.) Who cares if they are unhappy, it's not your problem, "Do not take someone else's unhappiness personally."

4) Stop Being Resentful

Do not force yourself to do the things you hate, and then resent doing it the whole time. If you are working at a job you hate, it's not anyone else's fault, you have free will, and it's a choice. So as long as you are staying at a job, or doing laundry, shift your perspective and be happy that you have free will. Be happy that you are healthy, be happy that you have a job, or laundry to do, etcetera. No one can force you to do something without your "free will consent"! So stop being bitter about it!

5) No Drama

DO NOT engage in any drama and/or judge anyone and their situation. This is about your happiness, not about how you can fix other people's happiness!

6) Boycott the News

Do not watch the news or read the newspaper. Those events are 98 percent negative and out of the realm of your control. If the world is coming to an end, a hurricane is coming, or the gas prices are going up, I promise you, someone will tell you about it.

Spiritual Rule #6
Pursue At Least One of Your Dreams

"When you follow your dream, life is easy. When you follow someone else's dream, life is unsatisfying. When you forget to dream, life is just plain confusing!"

This is important, so listen up! When you are pursuing at least one of your dreams, it will resonate with you on a soul level. When this happens you will begin to offer a different vibration, energetically, out into the Universe. Why does that matter? Because you are magnetized! Think of it this way, think of yourself as a human magnet. As a human magnet, the higher you vibrate the more powerful of a magnet you become, the lower you vibrate, the less powerful of a magnet you become. You begin to work with the Laws of Attraction, when your magnet is powerful, and things will begin to fall into place. Life gets easier, opportunities will begin to present themselves to you, it is amazing! Plus, let's face it, it's just fun! Please don't make excuses that you do not have time to pursue any of your dreams; it has been reported that people spend an average of eight hours a month on Facebook; use that time!

Here is an example:

I get asked a lot, "How did you end up in Hawaii?"
I say, "We sold everything we owned and we moved here!"
Other person, "Wow, I could never do that! But I sure would like to!"
"Why?"
"Why what?"
"Why couldn't you do that?"
Then comes the puzzled look, "Because I have a mortgage, a job, family, etcetera, etcetera ..."

You can always come up with a hundred excuses of why you cannot to do something, in fact, people think of excuses all the time! Why they can't move somewhere, why they can't change jobs, can't travel, or even relax. "There are too many things I need to get done!" I swear people's motto is, "I can't because ..." Let's be honest, people only make excuses to justify staying where they are at in life, or in a situation that they hate. They do it so they can feel better about not going after their dream, like somehow justifying it makes it acceptable. They make excuses because if they don't, everyone around them will tell them what a bad idea following their dream is! That's right, they will, and they did it to us too! If you are wondering, here is how we followed one of our dreams.

My husband and I decided that we needed to make a change. We had two houses and a construction company. The economy in the town where we lived began to get worse, and this was affecting the construction industry. Then my husband began experiencing heart pains. (Heart attacks happen when you are living a life that you no longer enjoy or you are stressed out all the time, in fact, it is quite common.) So my husband asked, "How about we move to Hawaii?" We discussed it and booked him a ticket. He left a week later to see what he thought and if we should move there. He made an appointment with a realtor and looked at housing in different neighborhoods. He also checked out job opportunities and talked with the local people he met along the way. When he came home he said, "Let's move!"

So we started filtering through all of our things, and had an auction (it is amazing to me how little you get for material items, after paying so much for them in the first place). That is definitely when my whole view on material things changed! We had so much stuff! Things we never used or had forgotten we had. We put both houses on the market and then we told family and friends. Oh jeez, they thought we had lost it! It's way too expensive there, what about jobs, what about the cost of living, what about us? Everyone was convinced that groceries were higher, gas was

higher, housing was higher and they had state income tax!
I was surprised at how many things they thought of, I was
surprised at the fear! But we were not afraid, and we had
moved within two months. We had no furniture, no jobs,
but we were in Hawaii!

Over the next three months we found jobs, we found furniture, and we made more money than before. Housing
was higher, gas was higher, food was about the same, but
clothes and car insurance were way cheaper. The pay was
higher, and the law requires that all employers provide you
with health insurance. All in all we are financially better off
and my husband's cholesterol went from three hundred to
under two hundred! There was a downside, however; you
are a six-hour plane ride away from the mainland, no more
road trips! Family was now far away, and it is expensive
to fly back and forth. In fact, moving to Hawaii isn't for
everyone; it does take some serious adjustment.

**Stop being afraid to follow your dreams. Stop being
afraid to make a big change! Stop letting material things
tie you down, financially or geographically.**

It is the most incredible feeling after so many years of having
multiple houses, cars, and things, to just free yourself, so
that you can go anywhere or do anything you want. I love
the freedom and I will never collect that much stuff again.
The crazy thing is after you move five thousand miles away
from your previous home of thirty some odd years, to an

island, you really conquer your fear! For the first couple of months I would think to myself, "What did we do?" But I adjusted to the initial shock that can sometimes follow change and I began to feel different, I began to feel like, "I can do anything, I can move anywhere. I am adaptable!"

Pursuing one of your dreams does not have to be a big move. For you it might be something like skydiving, taking a trip to Europe, going on a plane ride, or a roller coaster ride, enrolling in a Zumba class, learning French, visiting a friend, going to a spa, eating sushi, or volunteering at a homeless shelter.

Today I want you to make a plan to do something that you have wanted to do for a while, but you have not yet done, due to lack of money, lack of time, fear, family, whatever! I want you to check an item off of your "Bucket List" so to speak! People spend a lot of time and energy talking themselves out of doing something, or even planning to do something that they have always wanted to do. The reasons are endless! I don't have time, my kids are little, I don't have money, I will do that when I retire. Nope, you are going to "plan" it right now!

Dream time!

1) Pick something you have wanted to do for a while. Something that you are really excited about, or passionate about, something that you have made many excuses not to do, until now.

2) Set a date to start, to enroll, or try this new thing. The date cannot be longer than a year from today, unless it is a trip to Europe or around the world. But DO NOT set the date longer than five years out!

3) If money is an issue, find a jar, a piggy bank, or an empty bottle and label it. Put all of your change in the jar, everyday. Then, if you can, put the same amount of money in the jar every payday, five dollars, ten dollars, or fifty dollars, whatever you are comfortable with. You can even sell things, have a rummage sale, or pick up some extra hours at work, but make funding your excursion a fun focus.

4) Excuses are null and void here, they do not apply, and it is your mission to make this thing happen. It is not your mission to name a million reasons why it won't or can't happen, because we already know that you can do that just fine! This is a mission to overcome limits that you have set for yourself.

The purpose of this exercise is to help you to begin to restructure your old belief system.

This is not just a self-indulgent moment or exercise. Our belief system is what keeps us limited. When your belief system is supported by "I can't," or "It's just the way it is," it will affect aspects of your life that you are not even aware of. This is a pattern, and a way of life for many people, *it is learned behavior, not the way life works!* This exercise is designed to help your confidence grow. Experiences like this help you to become spiritually rich. You never hear people when they get older say, "I wish I would have accumulated more stuff!" They do, however, many times, regret not experiencing more of the things that life had to offer.

Spiritual Rule #7

Stop Looking For Happiness In the Future and Learn to Experience Happiness In the Present!

"Enjoy the moment. Everyone has become so busy looking ahead and worrying about their future, and looking at yesterday to see what went wrong, that they are forgetting to enjoy today."

When you are looking to the future for happiness, it means that you are failing to find it today. A lot of times this is an indication that bigger and better things are now defining your happiness. In other words, you have become "desensitized" to the little joys in life. Things like birthday parties, having lunch with a friend, enjoying the weather, laughing, or hearing someone laugh. When you are constantly looking towards the future to find happiness that is where your focus also lies; your thoughts become occupied by what lies ahead. The "now" becomes insignificant.

Experiencing happiness in the present requires:

1) Being more present!

Simply being more present and aware of what is happening around you at the time can open you to experiencing more happiness. People find it really hard to be present a lot of the time. They come home from work and they are preoccupied with thoughts of the day's events, or preoccupied with what it is they have to do tomorrow, or on the weekend. They rush to make dinner, all the while planning the future; who picks up whom, what chore needs done, what needs to be prepared for tomorrow, and so on. The next thing you know, today is yesterday and you weren't present at either place! Talk to your kids or spouse while looking "at" them. Not while you are looking at the stove, or at the computer, but by actually acknowledging their presence. They are your family and they deserve this from you. Observe what is going on around you, in your actual "physical" space, not your mental space, or your cyber space.

2) Have some down time.

Make a certain time during the day in which you have "down time." A good time to do this is during the evening when everyone is home. It should be consistent, so that your family and friends know there will be a time when you are approachable and mentally present for them if needed.

Down time is the time in which you unplug, do no work, or planning of the future. All family events, lunches, or dinners should be included in down time!

3) Unplug!

Put your cell phone and your computer away, and truly engage with others around you. Electronic devices are in full force trying to take over the world, and we appreciate that, but there is a time and place for everything. *It is important for you to unplug at some point during the day, every day, if you want to keep yourself present in the real world.*

4) Make lists for mental clutter.

This is a great way to help keep yourself in the present. People all have mental clutter. What is mental clutter? All of the things that you juggle around in your thoughts, in order not to forget things that need to get done, or things that need to be addressed at some point in the future. Instead of keeping them active in your thoughts, release yourself of the responsibility of remembering them by putting those thoughts down on paper. Then, make a habit of addressing them each morning. When you do this it allows you to free your mind, freeing it from the responsibility of being tied up with all of that information until morning. This allows your mind to relax into the present much easier, with much less multitasking to do.

Experiencing happiness in the present requires you to be present *mentally*! As you get older you will never remember that phone call you had to take, or the Facebook message you needed to answer, the email you had to answer, or what you were surfing for on the Internet. You will, however, remember the joke that someone told that made you laugh so hard, soda came out your nose.

Spiritual Rule #8
Negative Thinking Is Contagious...

"Negative thinking is contagious, do not infect
yourself with other people's thinking ..."

People worry all of the time about catching the flu, colds, or whatever big thing is going around that year. They don't want to be temporarily down and out, or inconvenienced with being physically "sick." Plus, they don't like the way it feels, and who can blame them? Since it worries them so much, they take proper precautions. They stay away from people who might be "contagious," they wash their hands and get flu shots. All the while they are preoccupied with all of these contagious things, they are letting one of the most "contagious" things, even more dangerous to your system, slip right under their radar. Negative thinking!

"What?" You might think, "Who cares! We are talking about my health here!" Well, you should care, that's for sure. Did you know that around 70 percent of the population are pessimistic thinkers, and that's just a fancy way of saying negative thinkers? Did you know that negative thinking has a *huge* impact on your physical and spiritual health? Did you know that it also has an impact on your money flow, and your life path? I bet the money part got your attention! Well it's true. Do you ever notice how you can be in a great mood, and someone else can come along and ruin your day because of their attitude? Then, the next thing you know you're ruining someone else's day? (Well you probably don't notice the last part.) Well it happens and it happens a lot! Why should you care? Because all of this negative thinking will have an impact in your life and on your health, and that's a fact!

What should you do about it? You can be more aware of how contagious negative thinking is. You can allow yourself not to be swayed by others, and not allow yourself to think everything is going to turn out crappy like they do.

You can stop watching the news!

Anyone else tired of consistently hearing negative things every single time that you turn on the news or open a newspaper? That is exactly why for the past ten years I have boycotted the news. But every once in awhile, I get a glimpse of it and it is an instant reminder of why I boycotted it in the first place! Government Shutdown, The Dow Plunges, More Deaths In Iraq, Bailout Money Where Did It Go? Tired of hearing it!

Now there are natural disasters that do occur, and those things are important to know about, because many of us have family and friends in various places. Even if you do not watch the news you will hear about those things, because somebody will insist on telling you about them. When people find out that I refuse to watch the news or read about it on the Internet, they say, "How are you going to know if anything bad happens?"

"Well," I say, "I can safely assume that according to the news, something bad is happening somewhere in the world, every minute, of everyday. If a tsunami is headed my way, well, we have a very good warning system!" (That warning system consists of alarms going off and fire trucks driving down the street yelling with a loudspeaker system to evacuate, which will wake you out of a dead sleep! See, no need for the news!)

With anything else that seems to be important, I can also safely assume that someone will tell me about it, and believe me they do. It is funny how many people feel the need to tell me the news, or any other bad thing they have heard that is now happening in the world, or with the economy. People I know, and people I don't know, it is a topic of discussion with everybody. Many conversations tend to revolve around all of the scary stuff that is happening out there in the world. People feel it is important, and you must know about it, and they also feel it is important to discuss. The funny thing is, if they had never told me about all of the "bad" things happening out there over the last ten years, my life would be exactly the same! Except for the fact that I would have many precious hours of my life back that would have seen relaxation, instead of having them wasted on all the stress that it caused me at that time.

So why should you stop watching the news? Because for the most part, it is wrapping you up in a tornado of negativity that is unnecessary. It is causing your own perspective to be tainted with hopelessness, fear, and negativity, and this will most definitely affect your life, and not for the better. You see, the news has gotten completely out of control, especially with the Internet. The news is now more utilized as a scare tactic, and as a way to influence the way people think. With anything from health scares (swine flu, bird flu, or influenza A), to the economy, to your safety, and how you should be so afraid of losing money, that you will agree with any solution placed in front of you (government bailout, Iraq war, etcetera) to make those feelings go away. Fear has been used as a form of manipulation for centuries; it is a very powerful and effective swaying tool. Especially when you can instill it into the masses, and what better way to do it than the Internet. Why the Internet? Because it is global, and you can reach many more people that way!

There are many positive things that happen in the world everyday, but who cares about that! Positive stories, they don't sell well, and they don't get your attention. Fear and destruction, now that gets your attention! From being subjected to constant negativity, people have become conditioned, without even knowing it, to be in a consistent state of fight or flight mode, they search for things that they have to protect themselves from. Isn't that sad? Negativity is so present around everyone's lives anymore, that it is considered common. It is more believable anyway; after all, we are surrounded by it every single day. What is the new flu this year? (Because every year the flu mutates into something different, which means more flu shots!) Am I going to lose more money? Is there going to be another war? Is it safe in that country? What about the terrorists? Is the economy going to collapse?

Your focus has an effect on your energetic system and whatever you focus upon will become more present in your life. The more you subject yourself to negativity, the more sensitive you become to it, and the world is a much scarier place. When you insulate yourself from unnecessary fear tactics, the world is not so scary, and life is not so scary. I have other things, during the day, that I would much rather focus my energy upon in my own life. I would much rather spend my spare time laughing, talking with my family, pursuing my dreams, and enjoying Mother Nature! Watch CNN? Please, I will have to pass and I suggest you do too!

Spiritual Rule #9
Do Not Take Other People's Unhappiness Personally

"Unhappiness can be like a virus spreading from one person, to the next person, to the next one, and so on. When someone is mean or rude to you, do not let their unhappiness infect your own life. If you are the unhappy one, please quarantine yourself so you do not infect others!"

Self-esteem for many people is determined by what other people think of them. It all seems to be tied together. Would you like everyone to like you? I am sure many of you would answer, "Yes!" Well good luck with that, because let's face it, no matter how likable you are, getting everyone to like you is next to impossible. You never want this to be a determining factor of how you *feel* about yourself. Why? People may like you today, you may tick them off tomorrow and many times you don't even know what you did, but hormones or hunger could certainly be involved. Because people change their minds like they change their underwear and here is what I mean.

Have you ever really thought about how people form their opinions? You need to look at it this way:

1) **People tend to form strong opinions based on their mood at the time.**

If they are happy their opinion is more on the positive side. If they are unhappy their opinion is more on the negative side. Just think about it. It is uncommon to hear someone who is in a great mood talk negatively about other people. However, if someone is in a bad mood, look out! They could find something wrong with Mother Teresa if they wanted to. They can lash out at anybody, or anything, without even being provoked and many times they will!

2) **People's mood is usually derived from the way their day went, and there are way too many factors that determine someone's day.**

For instance, perception, eating, weather, stress, hormones, money, all of these things can have an impact on someone's day. This is pretty self-explanatory, just look at how your day went today. What determining factors played a role in how your day is going, or had an impact on the mood you are in right now?

3) Do you really want how someone else's day went to spill over into your world?

Or have *any* kind of impact on your life for that matter? Um … I don't know about you, but for me that would be a big fat NO! People are way to wishy washy with their opinions about other people, and many times the people who feel the need to make it known what they think about you in the first place, are usually people who are not exactly in a position to be throwing stones.

We all have faults and flaws, that's just life! No one is superior and no one is immune to making bad choices. It is how you learn and grow from all of these different experiences, that is what life is all about. So the next time you hear what someone says about you, don't take it so personally. Change your view, and instead of taking it to heart and letting it spill over into your world, it should give you a little bit of insight into their world and you can think to yourself, "Well I know how your day is going!"

Spiritual Rule #10
Implement Change

"Things will never change if you never plan on changing them. Change requires action, action requires a plan, planning requires thought, and thought changes everything..."

Many times people have things in their life that they would like to change, yet instead of acknowledging what these things are, and fixing them, they silently stew. This stewing is in the back of their head most of the time, on a subconscious level, and stewing builds aggravation.

Changing little things in your life seems so easy, so why do you not do it? Well, because deep down you know the truth, and the truth is that it is not easy at all, in fact, it takes a bit of work.

1) You must first acknowledge that change is needed.

In order to acknowledge that change is needed, you must take responsibility. That alone can make you cringe; for most people this is very hard to do.

2) Then, there is problem solving.

Here is what I am sure many of you are thinking, "What! I do enough problem solving! I problem solve for everybody, my kids, my boss, I am tired of problem solving! I want to watch TV!"

3) Last but not least, you need to believe that your life is worth the work!

This is where it can get tricky. It is funny how much time and energy you can put into helping other people solve their problems, but when it comes to your own life, settling is just easier sometimes than initiating change. Change is not easy, but it is rewarding, and you have to want change more than you want to settle!

So here is a simple way to implement change:

1) Make a list: Make a list of five things that you would like to change in your life. Things like your job, your money situation, car, wardrobe, computer, shoes, a weight issue, hair, etcetera.

2) Write it on paper: Take five sheets of paper and at the top of each page, write one of the five things that you would like to change.

3) Address each piece of paper (or each issue): Under each heading you are going to give some thought to what it is that would help you resolve each issue, or change it for the better. For instance, say your weight is on page one, something that might make you feel better is losing twenty-five pounds, or maybe just looking physically fit, or more tone. If your wardrobe is page two and something you would like to see changed, something that might make you feel better is having updated clothes, or clothes that fit, or clothes that flatter your figure. If your job is on page three, what is it that you want? Do you want more flexibility, more money, a vacation, health insurance, to work closer to home? Be specific. You get the idea.

4) Make a game plan: Make a game plan to clear out the past and bring in the new. If your weight is an issue, part of your game plan could be getting a gym membership, or buying healthier food, or maybe running. *Change does not come about unless initiated!* If you are the one wanting change, and stewing, then you are the one that is going to need to be proactive. You can sit on the couch all you want and visualize losing weight, finding your soul mate, or working somewhere you love, but I guarantee that it will be coupled with the feeling of

aggravation, and that is self sabotage at its best! When you have a game plan, you begin to move towards being proactive, and you will begin to feel an *energetic shift*. This energetic shift is of great importance; **your intent shifts your energy,** and what it is you are projecting out into the Universe. This little shift is a major component to implementing change into your life.

5) Problem solve: Treat each item on your list as if your boss has given you a task to complete, and the task is to resolve each problem to the best of your ability. People can problem solve easier if they are asked to do it by someone else, for someone else's benefit. Write down steps you should take in order to get the results you want, as if you have to show your "game plane" to another person. Or even better, do this with a friend and do show it to another person!

6) Set a date: Put a date under each item of when you plan to start implementing change and moving toward your goal. You can use different dates and work on a different issue each week, or you can work on them all at one time, however you choose.

7) **Note your progress:** this is very important! Because many times people will do several things to initiate change and only remember a handful of them. If you

note all of the things that you do, it is like giving your self a pat on the back upon your review. Review your progress at the end of the month!

Spiritual Rule #11
Don't Let Fear Bully You

"If we lived in a world with no fear, then you would never discover the courage you have within."

Most people are really afraid of failure. So afraid, in fact, that it stands in their way of success. You might be thinking. "Failure of what?" Simple, everything! Failing in their relationship, failing in their marriage, failing at their job, failing to find happiness, failing in business, failing their kids, failing their parents, need I go on? People are so afraid of putting themselves out there because if they fail, the feeling is terrible, and sometimes that feeling can be hard to overcome. So it's just avoided all together, no failure, no terrible feeling.

Or if you do seem to gather up the courage to face your fears, everyone will promptly remind you that your chances of failure are HUGE! (Don't you love that?) The divorce rate is soaring, the economy is failing, the world is unstable, and governments are fighting, your chances of being successful are very limited. Then they follow up with, "Are you sure?" with a very concerned look on their face. As if you have just snatched up your sword and are heading out to slay a towering thirty-foot, fire-breathing dragon! (We will name the dragon "FEAR" for the sake of this chapter.) This dragon is very successful; in fact, "FEAR" has won all of its battles thus far. Suddenly you become terrified, "What if I do fail? All of those things are true, so true that no one else is being so brave." You think, "Maybe I shouldn't even bother in the first place? I changed my mind, I better go with the safer choice."

The problem with thinking this way is that **we as spiritual beings were created to experience**; we are built as natural explorers on a soul level. We want to live and we want to experience! So if you never put yourself out there, you are left with a spiritual void, a longing and unsatisfied feeling on a much deeper level, much deeper than you ever even think about.

Everyone is afraid of failing, but for some people, the desire to succeed far outweighs the fear.

That is really what sets many successful people apart from the not so successful people. It is not that they had no fear; it was that *their desire to succeed overpowered their fear of failing.* Here is an example of some famous failures:

1) Michael Jordan – Cut from his high school basketball team (bet they feel pretty stupid).

2) Walt Disney – He was fired by the editor of a newspaper for lacking in ideas. (Good thing that happened or no Disney. That would be weird).

3) Babe Ruth – Struck out 1,330 times.

4) Steven Spielberg – Applied to USC film school, but was rejected three separate times.

5) Donald Trump – Filed bankruptcy three times.

Those are just famous failures with good outcomes, but there are many, many ordinary people (I am sure many people who you know yourself) who have overcome their failures, and their fears, to become very successful in whatever it was they wanted to accomplish. It is important for you to know that most people are scared, they are scared of failing, but the people who overcome those fears and "jump off the high dive" so to speak, experience life the way it is meant to be lived. They feel a satisfaction of trying, down to their very soul. Even if they fail, they learn from that experience and usually will want to try it again. They begin to use any failures as learning material, as knowledge, in order to help them succeed.

"I've missed more than nine thousand shots in my career, I've lost almost three hundred games. Twenty-six times I've been trusted to take the game winning shot and missed. I've failed over and over and over in my life. And that's why I succeed!" – Michael Jordan

Spiritual Rule #12
Worry Less

"Worry less, enjoy more, because more often than not, things will work out anyway."

People worry way too much. The thing with worry is it doesn't change anything … or does it? Your reality is your perception, and your perception is formed by thoughts, beliefs, and experience. *Worry is a thought or concern based on fear that is accompanied by negative emotions.* These emotions accompany the thoughts and images in the mind, and are strongly felt in the body, forming the perfect storm of "worry."

Why should that all matter? Because of these two things:

1) Worry is generally a "concern" of an outcome of a situation that is not based on fact, and backed with no substantial proof that the outcome will indeed be negative. Your mind then goes straight to what you

don't want to happen (with no evidence that it will) and manipulates your thoughts to see how this negative event is a possibility.

2) The more you worry, the more the worry will solidify itself in your mind as a belief or fact.

Worry is based on fear.

People spend far more time thinking about every negative scenario that can happen to them or in their lifetime than they ever spend on a positive scenario that could possibly happen. In fact, negative thinking outnumbers positive thinking two to one, and most of the time it is a much higher ratio. Why? Because, it is easier (or more believable) for people to accept a negative outcome as a possibility than it is for them to accept a positive outcome as a possibility. Isn't that sad? Sad but true.

Worry is being too rigid in your thought pattern.

Worry is believing that there are limited outcomes to any given situation, and you spend most of your time focused on the worst possible outcome. Let the truth be told here, there are so many variables to every outcome that it would be mind boggling if you actually sat down and played out every scenario in your head.

Worry is based on negative thought and thoughts do become your reality.

Thoughts are energetic wave patterns that are sent out into the Universe and the wave patterns actually come together to form, and to become things. The energetic wave patterns of thoughts can be measured; this is quantum physics not metaphysics. Your thoughts go out into the Universe, and form your reality, *if you are not resistant to it*. In other words, if you can "feel" that it is a possibility, it is. When you worry, not only do you "feel" that the negative outcome is a possibility, the more you worry the more you obsess about it becoming your reality, the more energy you are focusing towards a potentially negative outcome. Then when it happens you say, "I knew this would happen, this is why I worry!" There, now you have more proof to justify your worrying for next time.

Worry is normal to an extent.

Worry is a normal emotion; in fact, everybody has experienced worry in his or her lifetime. It is okay to worry now and again as long as you do not obsess about whatever made you worry in the first place. Because more often than not, things will work themselves out. However, it is important when you allow worry into your thoughts, that you also allow worry to leave without forcing the worry to "park" itself there. It is unrealistic to never worry about anything, worry will happen on occasion and that's okay.

Just do not allow worry to come into your thoughts and hang out and loiter around, kick the worry out and occupy your thoughts with something else.

Break yourself of the habit of worrying.

People only seem to remember all of the times they worried that resulted in things turning out badly, just as they expected them to. Then they pocket that experience for a later date in order to justify more worrying. People very conveniently forget about all of the other times that their worry was unfounded. Here is a good trick to break yourself of this habit:

1) Take a piece of paper and write down every thing you are worried about right now. Anything you are worrying about, bills, school, a relationship, do not skimp here, write it all down.

2) Then seal this in an envelope and put it somewhere you will remember with a date to be opened in three months.

3) In three months when you open the envelope, you will most likely be surprised at all of the things you were worried about that turned out just fine. You will also probably have forgotten about many of the things that you put on the list. This trick is a good way to show yourself how things mostly do work out in your favor.

Spiritual Rule #13
Let It Go...

"Many times people find it very hard to break attachments! If something is not working after reasonable effort ... LET IT GO! When you are focusing your energy towards something that is not manifesting, it is "stuck," or hung up somewhere. Letting things go can be exhilarating! On an energetic level you will feel a lot lighter, because tension and resistance is then released."

Letting go is incredibly hard for people to do; however, learning to let go will be one of the most beneficial things that you will ever do for yourself.

When you let go, you must relinquish the need for control ...

What would your world feel like if you released the need for control over other people, and what they were doing, and you just let go? The responsibility is now off of your shoulders, and you are solely responsible for yourself, and the things that you do. Ah, doesn't it feel nice? Why? Because when you are trying to control a situation or an outcome of a situation that involves other people, you are working with resistance. How do I know this? Because, no one ever has to take "control" of something that is in the state of allowing, when something or someone is in the state of allowing it is flexible and ever changing. When situations, or people, are in a state of allowing they become adaptable. When you are trying to "control" a situation, or a person, or a person's behavior, the amount of energy it takes is exhausting. The worst part is **control is an illusion;** you will never be able to control anything, any situation, or anyone without consent. So in actuality there is no control, only consent!

When you let go, you are no longer forcing things to happen (pushing), you relax into a state of allowing (receiving).

When you are trying to force something to happen, you are working against the Universal Laws. Things do not like to be pushed. When pushed, energetically things tend to remove themselves or push back. You cannot push things into your life; the outcome is unfavorable to everyone and everything involved. Why? Because anything being pushed is in a state of resistance and when you are in a state of resistance there will be friction. When you relax into a state of allowing, then you begin to work with the Universal

Laws, there is no resistance, and there is no friction, there is only flow. When you allow yourself to *be in the flow of things*, your energy begins to "draw in and attract" instead of "push out and repel." This allows you to draw into your life things that you wish to happen, effortlessly. Allowing things into your life feels fantastic! It feels natural …

When you let go, it allows your energetic river to flow freely.

When you let go, you energetically allow things to flow in and flow out of your life freely. There are no stagnant ponds of energy in your system. This is so beneficial, because it means there is also a consistent flow of new energy streaming into your life. Energy that is fresh and clear, your system needs replenishment for nourishment and for growth. A consistent energetic flow also replaces any old, toxic energy, with new, vibrant energy. It allows your system a way to maintain a clean environment.

When you let go, you welcome change and let your resistance down.

Many people resist change because they know what it is they currently have, and they think, "What if it gets worse?" They never tend to think, "What if it gets a million times better?" So they resist change with all of their might. Change is inevitable and there are so many variables to any situation, things that have never even come across your radar. Since change is inevitable, resisting change does not stop it from happening; it only makes you feel more uncomfortable while it is happening. If you stop resisting change things may not turn out so bad, in fact, you may be pleasantly surprised! Change promotes growth and growth is a good thing. Resistance causes things to break or shatter.

When you let go, you break attachments.

Breaking attachments to something or someone can be incredibly freeing, and energetically you will feel so much lighter! When you are trying with all of your might to hold onto something or someone, you must consistently project a certain amount of energy outward, over and over again, in order to maintain the attachment. This takes a huge amount of effort on your part, especially if the attachment is primarily one sided. You must, in fact, double the amount of energy you would normally send out, because unless the energy is reciprocated, it will die out. In order to maintain this type of attachment, you are either knowingly or unknowingly committed to not letting it die out. Attachments do not promote growth, people use them to try and fill a spiritual void in their life. A spiritual void will never be filled with an attachment; your attention will only be temporarily diverted from it.

When you let go, you allow wasted and toxic energy to die out.

When you focus your attention towards any kind of drama going on in your life (which is extremely common), when you talk about it, discuss it, or give your opinion about it, you are energetically engaging the drama back. When you engage, or reciprocate in any way, it is like throwing fuel on an energetic fire, so to speak. Then, in many instances, you can watch this energetic fire burn out of control and injure innocent people along the way.

"When energy is sent out or focused in your direction, it can only maintain itself for a very brief time, unless (this is important) … it is somehow engaged upon."

If you are ever around negative people, and they direct a negative comment or action your way, let it go. Do not engage this behavior in any way, shape, or form. These are battles that are never won, they only appear to be won, when someone disengages himself or herself from the battle. Which is exactly what I am suggesting you do, disengage and let it go. Because if you do not disengage, anger, bitterness, and resentment, all of the things that come with engaging in this type of behavior, will then "park" itself in your energetic body. When these types of negative emotions "park" themselves in your body, they will then manifest in your cells, energetic or otherwise. Many times this is where manifestation of illness occurs.

> *"Energy that is focused upon you or in your direction has to have some energetic reciprocation or it will just die out."*

By all means … let it die out!

When to let go …

This is important! When you are focusing your energy towards something that is not manifesting, it is "stuck," or hung up somewhere. You will not be able to control it, force it, resist it, or manifest it into being, it will not happen! People really, really get stuck on this. When you shift your focus away from something that is not manifesting for you at the time, many times it will allow the energy that is "hung up" somewhere to work itself free. If that does not happen, removing your focus will usually allow another avenue to come to light. In either case:

If something is not working after reasonable effort … LET IT GO!

Spiritual Rule #14
Stop Saving Your Happiness For Special Occasions!

"Happiness is a gift from God that has been given to you. You can access it all day, every day if you choose, and live your life in complete and total bliss! Or you can choose to save it and only bring it out for special occasions."

Stop saving your happiness for special occasions!

I am shocked when I see people trying to suppress their laughter. They try and keep some type of composure, or hold their ground, by not laughing! Some people think that being an adult means being responsible, and being serious is acting responsibly, and laughter is not appropriate when you are being serious. Or there are also people who are upset or angry about something and the only way to show how angry or upset they are, is to make sure they repress any signs of joy. Otherwise, they will not make their point effectively! But who is really affected by repressing joy or laughter? The repressor is! So if you ever find yourself holding back a smile or laughter, well, stop doing that! That's just a roundabout way of wanting to control and resist your natural emotions. Who's that good for?

Laughter opens your heart chakra.

Opening your heart chakra is a very important part of working with the Universal Laws and raising your consciousness to a higher level. Chakras are energy centers where your physical body and your etheric body meet. Your etheric body is your "spiritual body." (You can learn more about your chakra system in my book Keys to the Spirit World.) When your heart chakra opens, you experience a feeling of happiness flooding over your body and into your soul. It is important for people to learn how to open and close their chakras; you need to exercise them just like you do your muscles. A very simple way to do this is by laughter; laughter opens your heart chakra naturally. If you never open your heart chakra, or suppress opening it by resisting laughter, then your heart chakra becomes harder to open each time. So remember to exercise you heart chakra, not only does it feel good to laugh physically, but it is very important for your heart and your spiritual body.

Laughter raises your vibration.

Everyone vibrates energetically, and laughter raises your vibration. Imagine that you are like a tuning fork, and your vibration can be measured on a scale from one to ten. Let's say that when you vibrate at a level ten, you energetically become a human magnet, powerfully drawing things into your life that you desire. On the other end of the spectrum, when you vibrate at a level one, your magnet has no power; with no power behind your magnet you will have a hard time drawing anything into your life. When you laugh, your magnet hangs out around levels eight to ten, and that could not be more beneficial! When you are offering a higher vibration, things become clearer, the Law of Attraction kicks in, and you naturally tap into your spiritual tools. Laughter is an easy way to raise your vibration.

Enjoy the little joys in life longer.

Sometimes the littlest things can bring you such joy. Those little things should be savored as long as possible, because the more you enjoy the little things, the more they turn into big things! Savor that feeling for as long as you can. It exercises the heart chakra and keeps your vibration high, it helps to keep your mood elevated, and it is good for you on a spiritual and physical level! I get so excited when I receive the artwork for my new book covers, that each time I get a new one I put them up as my screen saver, and on my phone. Then when I answer my phone or open my computer, I have a flood of happiness quickly fill my heart, no matter what mood I am in. Milk the little joys you have in life until you wear them out!

Spiritual Rule #15
Spend Some Time Creating Your Future!

"Always keep your focus forward, never in the past. If you focus on the past it holds you there. You cannot change the past, that is time wasted. When you focus forward and spend time creating your future, that holds value, it is time well spent!"

Many people ask me, "Where do you think that I should I be heading in life?"

To which I usually respond, "Well, have you given some thought to where you would like to be a year from now?"

Then comes the bewildered look, followed by the classic answer of, "No, guess I never really thought about it."

The reason I start with this question is because I like to know what their thought process is. This way I can help them learn what to do, instead of just giving them a quick fix. In my experience people tend to over complicate most things in life, and my rule of thumb is simplify, simplify, simplify! That being said, people need to spend more time clarifying their destination.

How on earth do you expect to get somewhere if you don't know where you are going? Many times people think that they need an expert to tell them what their skills are, or where they should be heading in life. But let's face it, who is the most qualified expert, someone who truly knows what your wants and needs are? You! You are underestimating your own skills! It is not as hard as you think to figure out what fits your current wants and needs; it just takes some time to think it through. More importantly it is FREE! "Excellent!" You are probably thinking, "Now how do I do that?" Well I am going to give you an easy six-step process and here it is.

Six steps to get you headed in the right direction:

1) First of all (again, make sure you do not overcomplicate this), it is a simple process of figuring out what your wants and your needs are. Very simple!

Do you want more time?
Do you need a vacation?
Do you want more stability?
Do you need less stress?

Take some time and figure these things out, and write these things down on a list. Do not rush the process; you might even want to carry a piece of paper around with you for a week, with the idea of completing this task. Because during the day is most likely when you will be able to identify what your wants and needs are. Then jot them down so you don't forget, and go about your day.

2) Spend a few minutes, hours, or weeks and imagine, what would your ideal day be like? Usually this pertains to work, so what would your ideal work day be like?

What kind of hours you would be working?
What time of day would you go to work?
When you would come home?
What type of people would you like to work with?
What type of environment would it be?
Would you be able to use your creativity?
Would it be more structured?

3) Next figure out what your ideal home situation would be.

Would your space be cleaner or more organized?
Would it be larger so that it didn't feel so claustrophobic?

Would you live in the same city, in the same state, or somewhere else?

Would you live with different people?

What feels good to you, or should I say, what feels better to you?

4) Take some time to visualize what it would *feel* like if your ideal day (home and work) was your current reality. *Really let this vision take hold.* Imagine going through a typical workweek, and what you would be doing every day. How does it feel? Ah ... it should feel really nice, because you have created this environment. If it doesn't feel right, start over again, until you get to the "Ah ... that feels good and way less stressful" part! Stay there for a moment, and enjoy the feeling, you should begin to feel your muscles relax and the stress melt away. Then allow yourself to feel the excitement of bringing some new changes into your life, and how good that feels. Breathe in your new life, and exhale the old stress.

5) Every morning or night (I prefer you do both), take a few minutes out of your day and visualize your future, your ideal day/life, a year from now. Spend some time enjoying that feeling everyday. Over time it will begin to feel like your comfortable place, you will enjoy being there. You do not have to do this for a set amount of time, it can be two minutes or twenty minutes, whatever you desire. A

really good time to do this kind of visualizing is during your "falling asleep" time. When you are lying in bed, just about to drift off to sleep, 90 percent of people spend this time going over the stressors of the day and predetermining the stressors of tomorrow. Biggest mistake people make! You are using some of the most valuable time, the alpha brainwave state, to manifest your stressors into your future reality. Let's use it more constructively, shall we?

6) Now that you have some detail and a direction in which way to go, start making choices that align with where you want to see yourself a year from now. Do not self-sabotage out of fear or worry and make choices that do not align with your new destination, out of fear or worry. Most of the time people are in their current situation, whether they want to believe it or not, because of fear and worry. So this is about trying something new and using a different approach. In other words, if you want to live somewhere else, begin to look for other places, or start saving some money, or both. If you want a different job, begin the process of scouting out what fits you better. Tell your friends what it is you are looking for, many times if you follow these steps the Universe will bring opportunity to you, and sometimes that avenue can be through friends or acquaintances.

Make choices that MOVE YOU FORWARD! Because most likely you are currently making choices that are keeping you right where you are, in your current situation.

All of this can be done in your spare time. Many times people do not think they have any spare time, but this is far from the truth. Most people just spend their spare time on Facebook, on the computer, on the phone, or watching TV. I know as well as the next person that when you begin to do any of those things, minutes turn into hours, hours turn into days and days turn into years ... you catch my drift!

Spiritual Rule #16
Get Rid Of Your Poverty Mindset!

*"Would you change your thoughts if you
knew that they would become a reality?
Just something to think about ..."*

Are You Cursed With A Poverty Mindset?

Well, first of all let's just disregard the word cursed, because
in over forty years of being a psychic I have never seen
a curse because they do not exist. (Unless of course you
have convinced yourself that they do, then, it is possible
in your world, but not in mine. Remember your reality is
your perception). However, I did know that it would get
your attention. Let's start with the basic issue, is there really
a poverty mindset? Absolutely! Now that you know that
there is such a thing as a poverty mindset, I am sure many
of you are wondering, "Well what is it? Do I have it? I need
to get rid of it!"

A poverty mindset is something like this: You are certain that all things related to money are driven by the economy and the economy is bad, so you are doomed to be poor!

For example, do you ever find yourself thinking any of these things?

1) I have always struggled in the past, I am struggling now, and I do not see how it is ever going to change!
2) There are not enough jobs out there, since no one else is getting one, that's a pretty good indicator that I won't get one either.
3) I can never afford anything that I want!
4) Those people (people with money), who live like that are different and have better skills, I never get a break!
5) I want to do XYZ, but I will never be able to because I will never have enough money.
6) I don't see things getting any better for me.
7) The economy is screwed, that means so am I!

It is so important for you to get this, and I really mean GET THIS! Your thoughts do become your reality! Now I am not kidding around here and people need to know this more then ever. *This concept is not metaphysics, this is quantum physics and it has been proven on a scientific level!* Secondly, there are more people making more money, every second, of every day, than you can possibly imagine! Now if it is just (physical) law that everyone's finances are dictated by, then this would not be possible! Thirdly, if this is all true, there must be something more out there that dictates our money flow!

Now if you pay close attention to Suze Orman, Rich Dad Poor Dad, Donald Trump, Bill Gates, Warren Buffet, or Sam Walton (I could go on), these people do not think of money in the same manner as 98 percent of the world. They know things, and they try and teach it to people, but for some reason it falls upon deaf ears. This currently does and will always separate the people.

Poverty mindset group (98% of the population):

1) They are sure they are a victim to how money flows to them, the economy, the stock market, gas prices, where they live, etcetera, and they will always be limited as to what flows in to their life. (There is another common poverty mindset word ... limited!)

2) They feel desperate for money; they never have enough, no matter how much they have, they always "need" more.

3) Money becomes a primary focus in their life. (Now that alone can be a huge problem, no matter how rich you are or how poor you are, the more your focus is on cash, I swear ... you will repel it!)

4) Money (or lack of it) is the reason, they believe, they are unhappy! They do not understand that happiness is a choice, not a side effect. There are some people in countries with no running water who are happier than people I know who have clean water anytime of the day or night, they just turn on the faucet and there it is! Amazing!

Now I am not making light of the money thing, you do need money to eat, pay the electricity bill and put a roof over your head. There have been many, many, years that I have lived paycheck to paycheck barely making it, with twenty dollars for the week to spend on groceries. Sometimes you need to work at a job that is low paying or that you do not like in order to make ends meet, but this should be viewed as temporary, not permanent, while you pursue your passion and your dream.

The other 2% of the population:

1) They know and truly believe that money is energy and it is constantly flowing.

2) They believe that there is more than enough to go around, that somehow, it will always work out.

3) They also believe that they are in no way limited to the amount of money that will flow into their life.

4) They do not always need to know how money will flow to into their life, but they know there are many possible avenues, and know somehow it just will.

5) They are not desperate for money, in fact, they are so focused and concentrated on following their passion, or their dream, that money becomes an afterthought, (even while they are sleeping in their car, or on someone else's couch).

6) Passion becomes the focus, even the addiction, and that will most definitely affect your money flow in the opposite direction, a very positive one, given time.

Did you know that many of the richest people in the world were born poor, and they were driven by their passion, (*this is very key here, they were not driven by money, but driven by what they loved doing*). Did you also know that many of them failed, or were so poor while they were on their journey, that they felt they were at rock bottom and the only way to go was up? That their only option was to succeed? Staying at rock bottom was not an option for them. Hmmm ... succeeding while poor. Yes, I like that option! Many of these people believe, truly believe, to the bottom of their soul that they are limitless, and that money is not restrictive. They believe their money flow is not tied to the economy or what other people are doing. Poverty mindset people feel very different, they look at money like it is in a clear cube, they know it exists, but it is untouchable. Do you see the difference? They feel to the very core of their soul, that money is untouchable! They know that it is there, they know that the money exists, but they do not feel that they could ever access enough of it in their lifetime, because they cannot *"see"* how it is possible.

Therein lies the difference. People who have acquired large sums of money in their lifetime (some of them started with less then you have right now), never needed to be able to *"see"* how it was possible in order to *"believe"* that it could happen to them. They just *"knew"* that it was, and therefore *"seeing"* it happen became their reality!

Spiritual Rule #17
Love Unconditionally

*"Love has amazing energetic power, thus has
an incredible effect on people. Just remember,
use your powers for good and not evil."*

Have you ever looked up the definition for love? Love is an emotion of strong affection that is based on kindness and compassion. Love is something that refers to a variety of emotions from passion and desire, to intimacy. Love can be a defined as romantic, or platonic, or it can be a strong passionate feeling about a desire or something you are compassionate about. Love can be many of these things and it can also be hard to define on some levels, but one of the ways love is never defined as is "conditional"!

Everyone wants to feel loved. Love is a major component to interpersonal relationships; family relationships, platonic relationships, or intimate relationships, love plays a major role. Love raises your vibration and opens your heart chakra. However, one thing that people do not know is that love is also energy, and as energy it must follow the laws of the Universe. This is important, especially for those wishing to have more love in their life. Energy needs to keep flowing or moving, in fact, it is important. With flow and movement, energy is consistently being replenished. With replenishment, old toxic energy is moved out and new vibrant energy replaces the old. Whatever energy you put out, must be replaced (unless you resist).

Love more.

Love is a very powerful energy! It has an amazing effect on other people, as well as your spiritual and physical body. The more you love the more you activate your heart chakra, which is a very important chakra to exercise. The heart chakra is tied to your higher consciousness, your vibration and your intuition. It also helps to balance all other chakras in your system. The more love you offer, the more you will also receive.

Love unconditionally.

Love as energy takes on a different form when you place conditions on your love. Love cannot be offered with anything other than *love in pure form*. When love is offered with conditions attached, the energy is no longer powerful, it is no longer activating your heart chakra, it becomes something else that you are sending out into the Universe, something else that will also flow back into your life. It becomes toxic love; love that is toxic to your system and others.

Love cannot be held hostage.

Love is not a form of manipulation; love is just that, love. Love in pure form cannot be held hostage. What do I mean by that? Holding love hostage is when you do not like someone else's behavior, so you decide not to "reward" him or her with your love. In other words, if they behave a certain way or do something you don't agree with, you make sure you do not show them any love. That is not love in its pure form; that would be toxic love. You see, love is not trying to manipulate someone else's free will and the choices they make; love is loving someone regardless of their free will choices.

Unconditional love.

When offering love, it is only offered in its purest form when it is offered unconditionally. Will people you love do things you do not agree with? Yes. Will people you love make mistakes? Yes. Will people you love even make bad choices? Yes. That is why we are here on earth as spiritual beings, to potentially do all of those things. Then hopefully we learn and grow, as a result of doing all of those things. To never encounter any disappointment from yourself, or others, is unrealistic. So it is most important for you to love unconditionally, regardless of choice, and regardless of mistakes, because we are all human, and as humans we sometimes make mistakes.

See your loved ones for who they are, not who you want them to be.

It is very important for you to truly *see* your loved ones for who they are, in order to offer pure love unconditionally. Why? Because it helps to eliminate disappointment and expectations on your end. Many times people do not see their loved one for who they are, rather they see them for who they wish them to be. ***Seeing the "potential" in someone does not make your loved one someone other than who they really are***. This implies that they are somehow less than, as a person, or they are somehow a disappointment to you, and others, at the current moment. It also implies there is a possibility, that maybe, someday, if they realize their "potential" they might be this really amazing person! However, for right now, they are just a person with great "potential." This really confuses people. When you see a glimmer of who you think your loved one could be in your mind, that glimmer can take on a whole life of its own and create a whole new being that does not even exist! This often results in disappointment and anger. ***Appreciate your loved ones for who they are not for who you wish them to be.***

Do not mistake manipulation for love.

Pure love cannot be used as a manipulation tactic, toxic love can be. Do not mistake anyone who wishes to change who you are or your behavior in exchange for his or her love, as love in pure form. In fact that is not love at all, it is just manipulation in disguise.

Pure love is offered unconditionally, with no strings attached. There are no guidelines you must follow, or "potential" you must live up to; you are just loved for the simple fact that you exist!

Love more.

Spiritual Rule #18
Take Care of Yourself Physically

"It doesn't matter how good of a driver you are if you fail to maintain the vehicle you are driving in. You must maintain spiritual and physical balance in order to perform to the best of your ability. If ignored, you will end up parked along the road somewhere with your hazard lights on."

Balance is key as spiritual beings living in a physical world.

We are spiritual beings, but we do live in a physical world, and this is also important. Your spiritual self is most definitely a huge part of your existence, in fact, it is your existence. However, when living in a physical world there are some other things to consider. One of the things is, your physical body is the vehicle you are given in order to maintain your existence on earth, here in the "physical world." If your vehicle is not properly cared for and maintained, your vehicle will most likely break down at some point in time, potentially affecting the quality of your journey and even the length of your stay.

Many things dictate the way your body operates physically. The spiritual aspect is very important; however, we have covered a lot of that elsewhere in this book. So for the sake of this chapter we are going to cover the physical side here.

Eat right.

When you think of a vehicle or a piece of machinery, you understand that it is important for those things to have oil and gas to allow all of the internal parts of the vehicle to run smoothly. When you look at plants and vegetation, you understand that it is important for the plants to have rich soil full of nutrients, sunlight, and water. Having these things allows the plants to grow and thrive, and with that comes the ability to weather the environment. Your body is no different. You need to make sure that you provide your vehicle, or your body, with food filled with nutrients, and with water. It is important to keep the things that you put into your body as healthy as possible. When you maintain a healthy body, it becomes strong and resilient. This gives your body the ability to weather an environment of toxins or illness rather well. Eating well and making sure you have the right vitamins and minerals should be a part of your physical balance.

Exercise.

Your body is blessed with over six hundred fifty muscles! Your body is a wonderful piece of human machinery. Do you know what happens to machinery when you let it sit for long periods of time without any use? Things become brittle, parts begin to rust, particles accumulate on the surface, and oils dry up. If you allow this to happen with a piece of machinery, when you decide that it is useful again and go to operate the machine, what do you think is going to occur? It is not going to operate well. Again, your body is no different. Your muscles are meant to be used, and in order to use them, they must be maintained. Exercise should also be a part of your physical balance.

A machine is a device consisting of fixed and moving parts that modifies energy and transforms it into a more useful form.

What a wonderful piece of machinery you have, your very own body! Take care of it and appreciate it inside and out. Do not neglect it, and then get frustrated when it is operating at a less than optimal level. Your body is meant to be a useful vehicle that makes your very existence in the physical world possible!

Spiritual Rule #19
Listen To More Music

"When you need a natural mood elevator put on some music. Music makes the soul smile."

Music elevates the soul vibrationally.

Music reaches you on a deeper level then you may even realize. There is a reason music is connected with Angels in the spirit world. Music touches you and elevates you on a soul level. When you are listening to music that you enjoy, it elevates you not from the outside in, but from the inside out! This is a huge benefit to your spiritual and physical being. Because when it resonates with you on a soul level, the chemistry of your body actually changes.

Music is a good distraction from worry.

It is hard to worry and stress out about something when you are listening to music. Your body wants to feel the music, you find yourself wanting to sing the words. You cannot sustain worry and enjoy music at the same time for very long. The stronger one of the two will eventually take over and naturally you will gravitate towards what makes you feel better.

Music affects your emotions, therefore, is a natural mood elevator.

Because of the physical effects music has on your body chemistry it also has an effect on your brain. There have been many studies done on how classical music affects your brain function and emotions. But this actually applies to all music that elevates your soul, or that you personally like. It is a natural mood elevator, without the use of chemicals!

Music research shows it elevates memory, learning, and is good for your cardiovascular system.

There has also been much research done over the years to show how music is good for memory, learning, and your physical body. Music tends to relax the physical body when needed and motivates the brain and the physical body when exercising. Music activates within you personal motivation and strength. They have actually tested this by taking two groups of people exercising, one group listened to music and the other did not. The group listening to music out performed the group that was not, quite a bit. Music has been shown to relax the body, showing changes

in heart rate and heart rate variability promoting cardio health. There have been mountains of research showing the effects music has on your memory and learning capacity. I personally have never met anyone
who did not like music of some kind. From the dawn of man it has been enjoyed. There is proof all over the place that music is beneficial for you on a spiritual and physical level, all pointing towards one thing.

Listen to more music!

Spiritual Rule #20
Give and Appreciate

"I love that I can find clean drinking water most everywhere that I go, I love that I do not have to sew, or make my own clothes. I love that I can go into a store and have a million things to choose from to eat without having to grow it, or walk thirty miles for it. We are so blessed!!!"

This chapter is about giving to others and acknowledging what you already have (because let's face it, most days you take for granted that you have a home, running water, and food to eat). Well it is time to wake up and smell the coffee, so to speak!

Today is a day of appreciation. For today, I want you to take the focus off yourself and what you don't have and start looking at other people, and how you might be able to help them. Many people are in the same boat as you are, and many people are in a situation that is much, much, worse! Yes, I said it, much worse! Because if you are reading this book you are not struggling to find clean water to drink; need I say more? This day is not about how you need help, but how you can help one other person, a pay it forward kind of day!

Anyone can do this; you can give money, or time. Here are some ideas:

1) Give money to someone in need. You can give $1, $5, or a $100, it doesn't matter. Not to your kids, or family, this is about giving to someone in need with no ties attached and no need for acknowledgement about the giving. You could tip someone more than usual, or donate some money to charity. However you wish to do it.

2) Give some of your time. If you are a professional, donate fifteen minutes or an hour of expertise. Donate babysitting time or volunteer!

3) Give clothes or items. There are almost always items around your house that you do not use, wear, or need. This is almost always true with toys and clothes. You can give them to a shelter, or to someone moving, toys for tots, Salvation Army, whatever!

4) Give food. Give to someone in need of food, a dinner, or a can of soup. Give whatever you can provide.

A lot of times people feel that a can of soup or a dollar is so little that it does not mean much. This is the wrong perspective; this day is about the intent of helping someone in need, not how much you can give. The intent of helping people is very powerful! Can you imagine if even half of the population did this tomorrow? Can you image the energetic effect that it would have, the love behind the giving and receiving? Powerful!

REMOVE ALL JUDGEMENT!!!! This is not your time to judge why anyone else is in his or her current situation! It is your time to find love in your heart and give from there ... that is all ... nothing less, nothing more. Giving should just be that, giving!

Spiritual Rule #21
Embrace the Power You Hold

"Know there's more, because there is ... Go after what you want, because you can ... Live your dream life, because you're meant to ... Don't settle, because everyone else does."

You are not a victim of life! So don't act like it!

The strong and the weak are not made somehow genetically different or spiritually different from one another. The difference between the strong and the weak is that ***the strong utilize the power they have, and the weak deny they have any power at all!*** You were born with gifts and abilities, use them. You were created with spiritual tools, use them. What you don't know, learn, and what you learn, teach!

Embrace the power you hold!

You have the power to become who you want to be.

You have the power to be successful.

You have the power to thrive.

You have the power to keep going.

You have the power to resist.

You have the power to stop.

You have the power to fail.

You have the power to give up.

You are blessed with power. It's up
to you how it will be used.

You are powerful beyond belief!

Appendix 1
21 Commandments To Your Happiness!

1) I understand I am a reflection of my choices.

2) I will not let my relationship status define my happiness.

3) I have removed all contingency clauses previously attached to my happiness.

4) I release myself from all expectations.

5) I will not hold anyone else responsible for my happiness.

6) I will always be pursuing at least one of my dreams.

7) I will experience happiness in the present.

8) I will protect myself from other people's negative thinking.

9) I will not take other people's unhappiness personally.

10) I will implement change.

11) I will not let fear bully me.

12) I will worry less.

13) I will let things go.

14) I will stop saving my happiness for special occasions.

15) I will spend time creating my future.

16) I will rid myself of a poverty mindset.

17) I will love unconditionally.

18) I will take care of myself physically.

19) I will listen to more music.

20) I will give and appreciate.

21) I will embrace the power I hold!

Appendix 2
Do You Feel Like You Are In a Rut?

What in the world is happening? I am encountering many, many people who are experiencing the same thing around the world. It is a flurry of undirected energy! I have friends and colleagues who are wondering, what's this all about? I am normally focused, I can usually get things done in a timely manner, but lately I feel like I am going in circles!

This can happen when you are feeling a flurry of undirected energy and it can result in people feeling like they are in a rut. I have received quite a few emails asking for me to elaborate a bit more on some steps to take when you feel this way. So here are some easy steps that you can take, broken into two different categories. Why two categories, you may wonder? The first one will be for linear thinkers; these people like to think things through on a more practical level instead of spiritual. The second category is for the more spiritually based thinkers. Now keep in mind that it is most effective if you just do all of these things, or at least some of the things from each category.

Linear Based Thinkers:

1) Educate yourself more on the relationship between energy and money. Money is energy! Most well-known financial advisors like Suze Orman and Rich Dad Poor Dad talk about money as an energy. This is why money is also referred to as currency.

2) Shift your perspective and take your power back. You are not a victim unless you allow yourself to be!

3) Get rid of the mind clutter! What is most important to you at this time of your life? Do you need to get bills paid, more freedom, more time, etcetera. Then create a list and prioritize the list from top to bottom, most important things first. Focus on tackling the things at the top of your list, then working your way through to the bottom. Many people just feel like they have a barrel full of issues to deal with and no organization, so they have no idea where to start. When you have no organization this leads to something that I like to call "mind clutter." The problem with mind clutter is that it will leave you feeling really overwhelmed, and with no clear starting point, it's just easier to put things off over and over again. Then your barrel gets really full and that can lead to major stress or anxiety.

4) Prioritize yourself and implement the 75/25 rule. What is the 75/25 rule? You commit 75 percent of

your free time focusing on yourself and 25 percent of your free time helping others. Why? Because most people commit more free time to helping others than they commit to making their own life better. When you fly on an airplane, during the safety instructions the stewardess will say, "Make sure to put your own oxygen mask on first before you help others, in case of emergency." It is similar to this, you cannot help other people when your own life is in shambles, or you are unhappy. Why? Because, even though you might beg to differ, it is not effective, period! It is way more effective to help others when you have it together. Let's face it, how well would you take relationship advice from your cousin who is an unhappy, self-proclaimed, serial dater? That advice is not nearly as effective as the advice coming from Grandma and Grandpa who have been married for forty-five years! Especially when it seems that they have truly experienced the ups and the downs of a relationship and how to deal with them in a successful manner. If you are the cousin, then let's get it together!

Energetic Development (Spiritually Based Thinkers):

1) Break Inertia! What does that mean? Do something different, switch up your daily routine. If you are sluggish, get moving, if you are hyperactive, be still. For instance, if you normally exercise at night, then start doing it in the morning for a while. If you don't exercise

at all, then take a walk, jog, ride a bike, or play tennis twice this week. If you normally do house work in the evening, do it in the morning. Break boring repetitive patterns and choose a challenge. ***Power is seldom developed by clinging to security,*** give up being safe, and your power chakra (your third chakra) will awaken more quickly!

2) Avoid invalidation and criticism from those who do not understand your situation, especially if you are a sensitive person who takes things to heart. When you are undertaking something new and uncertain, invalidation and criticism can be an instant power crippler!

3) Make sure your energy travels in a complete circuit! In other words, what you put out comes back; remember the 75/25 rule.

4) Both effort and resistance are tiring and wear your energy down. That is a sign that your power is not flowing harmoniously. *When you find yourself straining with effort, stop!* Think about what you are doing and imagine doing it without effort – smoothly and enjoyably. (Morning meditation.)

5) Morning meditation! This is really important, and believe me, I have gotten busy myself and skipped it. Boy is that an instant reminder of why not to skip morning meditation; I think it's as bad as skipping breakfast!

Take a minute, two minutes, or five minutes, whatever you want, and sit quietly in a chair. When you do this I want you to imagine your day going exactly the way that you want it to. (See Appendix 3.)

6) Attention … attention focuses energy! Pay it when it needs to be paid and give it to yourself. Notice where it goes, the rest of the energy will surely follow.

7) Grounding brings us into the present. Of course there is meditation for grounding, but you can also go jogging, power walking, or do ab workouts.

You will probably not do all of these things overnight, but pick the ones that resonate with you and start doing those things right away. You will surely begin to notice a difference!

Appendix 3
What Is Meditation?

Meditation is a practice of sitting quietly while regulating your breath using intone mantras or visualization in attempts to harmonize your mind, body, and soul.

Why is this important? Because meditation is really effective in clearing out mind clutter as well as energetic clutter. It is knocking out two birds with one stone so to speak, on a spiritual and physical level. You clean your house, take showers, eat right, and maintain your physical health by getting the proper rest, etcetera. Well, equally important to your physical and spiritual health, is to keep your mind and your energetic field as clutter free as possible. This will allow you to operate at your most efficient level.

Meditation synchronizes brain wave patterns.

There have been extensive studies done on meditation over many, many years, and the most interesting findings seem to show in the EEG measuring of brain wave patterns. During your waking consciousness, brain waves are random and chaotic. The brain usually operates with different wavelengths from the front to the back of the brain, and from hemisphere to hemisphere. Meditation changes this drastically. Subjects in meditation show increased alpha waves, and these waves continue to increase throughout the duration of the meditation. Also, the front and the back of the brain begin to synchronize as well as the left and the right hemispheres. In other words, the different areas of your brain begin to work together synchronistically! After a few months, this integration in the brain is not just noticed during the meditation state but during daily activity as well.

Meditation has spiritual and physical health benefits.

Meditation has also been linked to lowering blood pressure and helping with anxiety and depression, just to name a few. Not to mention the spiritual aspects of raising your vibration, intuitive development, and raising your consciousness.

Meditation Exercise

I have designed a meditation exercise to help you work more efficiently with the Universal Laws. I suggest doing some type of meditation at least once a day. I personally recommend meditating in the morning if you only have time for one meditation. Morning meditation, I have noticed, definitely sets the tone of your day.

Before you begin, find a quiet place where you will not be disturbed. You will be using a chair for this meditation, so find a comfortable chair to sit in, then place both feet flat on the floor.

1) Define what it is that you want to achieve in your meditation. This is a very important step whether it is calmness, joy, better health, or happiness; whatever it is that you desire. It is very important because intent is what actually creates anything whether it is in the spiritual or physical realm.

2) Sit comfortably in a chair or in an upright position in a quite place.

3) Close your eyes and concentrate on your breathing. Slow your breathing to a relaxed state.

4) Once your breathing is rhythmic, concentrate on relaxing all of the muscles in your body.

5) Imagine that your spine is like a string on a musical instrument. Imagine that this string or cord attaches all of your chakras together, from your root chakra to your crown chakra.

6) Visualize this string or cord vibrating. Imagine that you are in control of how fast or slow the vibration is. Next

raise this vibration to the highest level of vibration that you can achieve.

7) When you are vibrating at a high level, imagine that you can see a river above your body. Imagine that this river is the river of the Universe. This river of the Universe contains all of the Universal energy.

8) Then visualize that you are attaching your energy to the Universal River. When you attach your energy with the Universal River, feel yourself flowing in harmony with the Universal Laws.

9) From that state imagine whatever it is that you desire being attracted to you. Imagine that your desires are coming to you as if you are a human magnet.

10) Remain in this state until you feel a sense of completion, then release this image into the Universe.

You should not set a time limit on how long or short your meditation should be, just do what feels right. For many people it will change each day, some days it might be twenty minutes while others it might be two minutes.

Special Note From Me To You

Aloha Soul Seeker!

Since writing my books, I've now shifted my focus in another direction...teaching.

I love it!

Since then, I've had a flood of students coming my way who are excited to take this journey with me. And we've had such great success. :)

I'm gearing up for even more teaching this year, and because of that I've decided to change my "teaching structure" a bit to better suit my students.

So here's what's I've got going on:

1) I'm currently adding new material. This will include new classes, meditations, etc.

2) For the first time ever, I'm now offering my Psychic Ability Class year-round. This means no more waiting, you can enroll all year!

This class has been more helpful to people than I ever would have imagined.

The reason I developed this class frankly, was demand, people wanted to learn more. They were ready to learn more.

The reason I personally think this class is SO important is, I consider this class a foundational class.

A class that creates a solid foundation for you to build on. Especially if:

* You're learning to develop your psychic senses.

* You currently feel blocked, or stuck.

* Or you're interested in advancing your skill and working with your spirit guide, spirit communication, healing, etc.

If you are one of those people. If you're ready, and interested in advancing or learning more, you can find out more information here:
Psychic Ability Class
https://www.psychicabilityclass.com/

If not, that's fine too! I have a very special gift just for you...

MY Favorite Meditation & My Gift To You!

The CHI Meditation is specifically designed to help you *raise your vibration...*

DOWNLOADED OVER 11,000+ TIMES!

This meditation is one of my personal favorites...

CHI MEDITATION. A meditation with a powerful purpose!

This meditation was channeled and given to me by my council. They call it the **CHI MEDITATION**, and if you are on a spiritual journey of your own, it's definitely one you will want to add to your spiritual tool box. It's specifically designed to do several things while your spiritual body is trying to *adjust* to the **NEW CONSCIOUSNESS ERA.**

This mediation is designed to:

RAISE YOUR VIBRATION. While the earths vibration is raising and ascension energy is upon us, it is very important to learn how to raise your own vibration. You need to be able to adjust your own vibration to match this new energy. This allows you the ability to *find balance between your physical and spiritual bodies*, and *clarity when working with Universal Energy*. This ability will affect your overall health and well-being.

STRENGTHEN YOUR ENERGY FIELD. As this ascension energy is becoming more powerful, it is more important now than ever before to keep your own energetic strength up. To keep your energy field strong. This allows you to keep a *strong spiritual immune system* so to speak.

OFFER ENERGETIC PROTECTION. Our two worlds are essentially coming closer together. While the earths energy is raising higher in vibration, the spiritual veil is thinning. This means it's very important to practice energetic protection. This allows you to feel more *energetically stable*.

Teach you how to connect with your spiritual body in a very powerful way!

DOWNLOAD NOW!
http://keystothespiritworld.com/chimeditation

Author Bio:

I was born looking at the world differently than most everyone else around me. The funny thing is I thought everyone was like me. It wasn't until I got older that I realized...I was born with a very special connection to the spirit world. This connection has allowed me to access things you can benefit from. Lots of information on how things work in the spiritual realm,

how things work energetically in the physical realm, as well as how this information can help you to enhance your life and help you to live the best life possible. I was gifted with this ability with a purpose, to teach others. To show you that you have some of these same abilities, and to simplify the process of using these spiritual tools and gifts you were born with in a way that fits into your everyday life.

—Jennifer O'Neill

Connect with the Author

Twitter:
@keystothespirit

Facebook:
https://www.facebook.com/JenniferONeillAuthor

Join Jennifer's Spirit Community:
Higher Purpose Learning Group
https://www.facebook.com/groups/405615596232631

Website:
http://keystothespiritworld.com/

YouTube Channel (over 100+ videos):
http://pxlme.me/OqRDaX10

iTunes (over 140+ Podcasts):
http://pxlme.me/4fnIcpSn

Made in the USA
Columbia, SC
11 May 2018